CW01192187

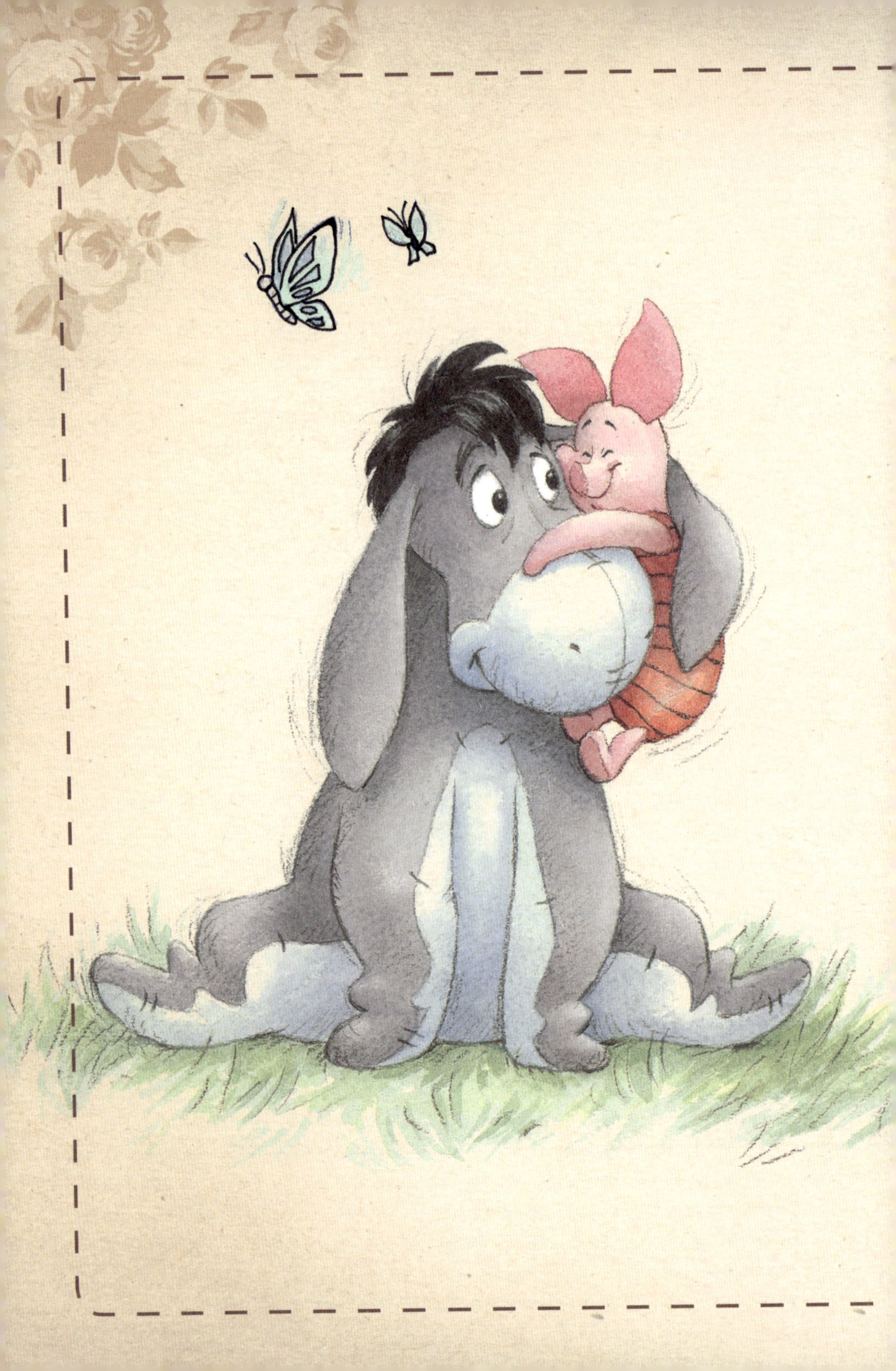

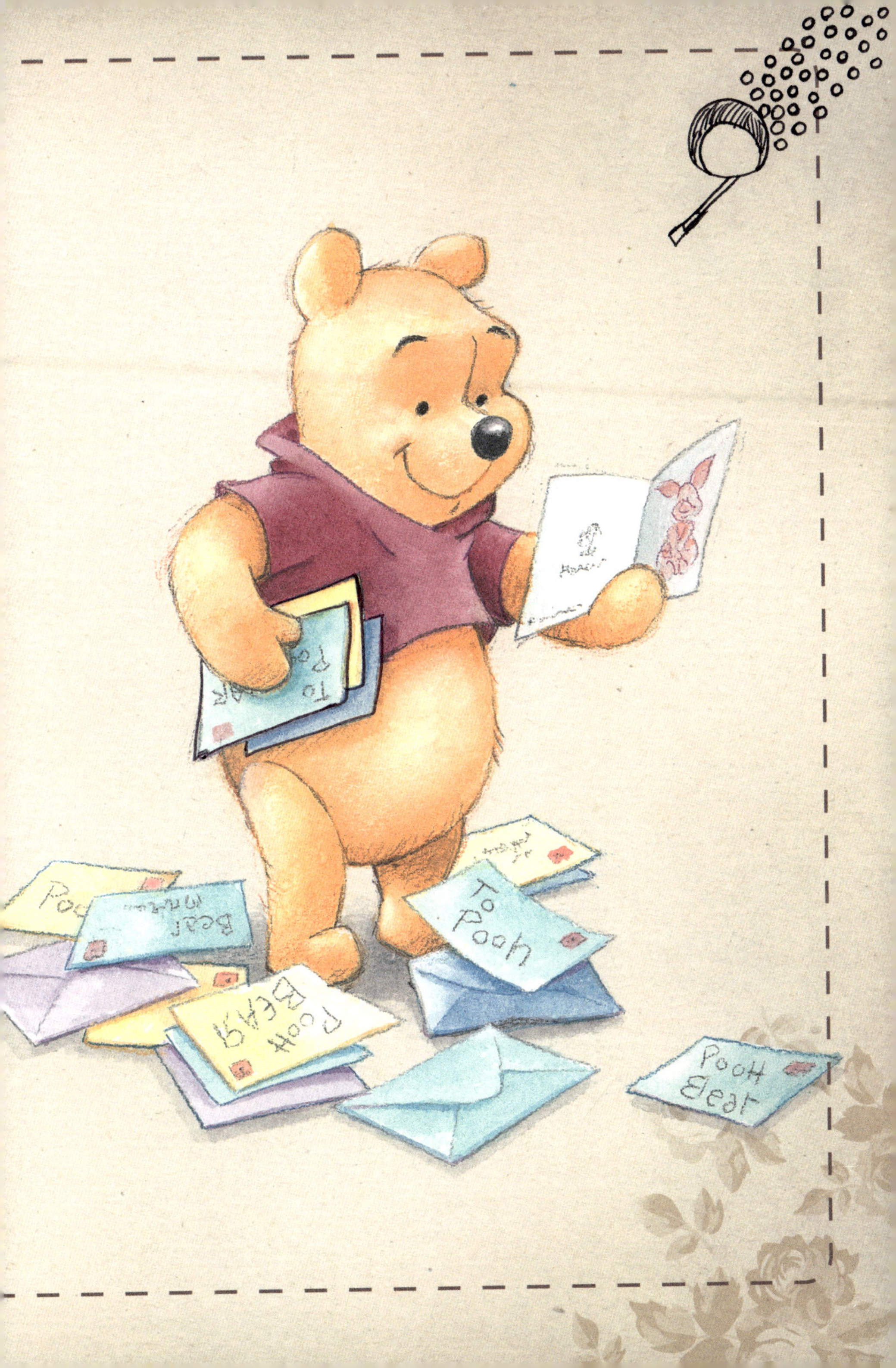
To Pooh
Pooh Bear

January

To do... Save money.

Don't forget...

Notes...

Monday
31 Morning 10:00 - work.

New Year's Eve

Tuesday
1 Night 21:30 - work

New Year's Holiday (UK & Republic of Ireland)

Wednesday
2

Holiday (Scotland)

Thursday
3

Dec 18 / Jan 19

Friday
4

Saturday
5

Sunday
6

Notes

Monday
7

Tuesday
8

Wednesday
9

Thursday
10

Friday 11 — PART A Practical Exam 9:00 - 12:00 [Chem/Bio/Phy] B 134 arrive 8:30 am

January

Saturday 12

Sunday 13 — Holiday work

Notes

Monday
14

Tuesday | Biology — pm — 40 mins   Holiday work
15

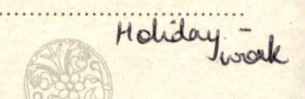

Wednesday | Chemistry — am — 40 mins
16 | Physics — pm — 40 mins

Thursday
17

January

Friday
18

Saturday
19

Sunday
20

Holiday
- work

Notes

Monday 21

PART B (Section 1 and 2)
Practical Exam
(9:00 - 10:30)

Tuesday 22

Wednesday 23

Thursday 24

Jan/Feb

Friday
1

Saturday
2

Sunday
3

Notes

Monday
4

Tuesday
5

Chinese New Year
Wednesday
6

Thursday
7

February

Friday
8

Saturday
9

Sunday
10

Notes

Monday
11

Tuesday
12

Wednesday
13

Thursday
14

St. Valentine's Day

February

Friday
15

Saturday
16

Sunday
17

Notes

Monday
18

Tuesday
19

Wednesday
20

Thursday
21

February

Friday
22

Saturday
23

Sunday
24

Notes

March

To do...

Don't forget...

Notes...

Monday
25

Tuesday
26

Wednesday
27

Thursday
28

Feb / Mar

Friday
1

St. David's Day (Wales)

Saturday
2

Sunday
3

Notes

Monday
4

Tuesday
5

Wednesday
6

Ash Wednesday

Thursday
7

March

Friday
8

Saturday
9

Sunday
10

Notes

Monday
11

Tuesday
12

Wednesday
13

Thursday
14

March

Friday
15

Saturday
16

Sunday
17

St. Patrick's Day (Ireland)

Notes

Monday
18

St. Patrick's Day Holiday (Ireland)

Tuesday
19

Wednesday
20

Thursday
21

March

Friday
22

Saturday
23

Sunday
24

Notes

Monday
25

Tuesday
26

Wednesday
27

Thursday
28

March

Friday
29

Saturday
30

Sunday
31

Mothering Sunday (UK) / Daylight Saving Begins

Notes

April

To do...

Don't forget...

Notes...

Monday
1

Tuesday
2

Wednesday
3

Thursday
4

April

Friday
5

Saturday
6

Sunday
7

Notes

Monday
8

Tuesday
9

Wednesday
10

Thursday
11

April

Friday
12

Saturday
13

Sunday
14

Notes

Monday
15

Tuesday
16

Wednesday
17

Thursday
18

April

Friday
19

Good Friday (UK) / Passover (Pesach)

Saturday
20

Sunday
21

Easter Sunday

Notes

Monday
22

Easter Monday (UK & Republic of Ireland)

Tuesday
23

St. George's Day (England)

Wednesday
24

Thursday
25

April

Friday
26

Saturday
27

Sunday
28

Notes

May

To do...

Don't forget...

Notes...

Monday
29

Tuesday
30

Wednesday
1

Thursday
2

Apr/May

Friday
3

Saturday
4

Sunday
5

Notes

Monday
6

May Day Holiday (UK & Republic of Ireland)

Tuesday
7

Wednesday
8

Thursday
9

May

Friday
10

Saturday
11

Sunday
12

Notes

Monday
13

Tuesday
14

Wednesday
15

Thursday
16

May

Friday
17

Saturday
18

Sunday
19

Notes

Monday
20

Tuesday
21

Wednesday
22

Thursday
23

May

Friday
24

Saturday
25

Sunday
26

Notes

June

To do...

Don't forget...

Notes...

Monday
27

Spring Holiday (UK)
Tuesday
28

Wednesday
29

Thursday
30

May / Jun

Friday
31

Saturday
1

Sunday
2

Notes

Monday
3

Tuesday
4

Wednesday
5

Thursday
6

June

Friday
7

Saturday
8

Sunday
9

Notes

Monday
10

Tuesday
11

Wednesday
12

Thursday
13

June

Friday
14

Saturday
15

Sunday
16

Father's Day

Notes

Monday
17

Tuesday
18

Wednesday
19

Thursday
20

June

Friday
21

Longest Day

Saturday
22

Sunday
23

Notes

Monday
24

Tuesday
25

Wednesday
26

Thursday
27

June

Friday
28

Saturday
29

Sunday
30

Notes

July

To do…

Don't forget…

Notes…

Monday
1

Tuesday
2

Wednesday
3

Thursday
4

July

Friday
5

Saturday
6

Sunday
7

Notes

Monday
8

Tuesday
9

Wednesday
10

Thursday
11

Friday
12

Holiday (Northern Ireland)

Saturday
13

Sunday
14

Notes

July

Monday
15

Tuesday
16

Wednesday
17

Thursday
18

Friday
19

July

Saturday
20

Sunday
21

Notes

Monday
22

Tuesday
23

Wednesday
24

Thursday
25

July

Friday
26

Saturday
27

Sunday
28

Notes

August

To do…

Don't forget…

Notes…

Monday
29

Tuesday
30

Wednesday
31

Thursday
1

Jul/Aug

Friday
2

Saturday
3

Sunday
4

Notes

Monday
5

Holiday (Scotland & Republic of Ireland)

Tuesday
6

Wednesday
7

Thursday
8

Friday
9

Saturday
10

Sunday
11

Notes

August

Monday
12

Tuesday
13

Wednesday
14

Thursday
15

August

Friday
16

Saturday
17

Sunday
18

Notes

Monday
19

Tuesday
20

Wednesday
21

Thursday
22

August

Friday
23

Saturday
24

Sunday
25

Notes

September

To do...

Don't forget...

Notes...

Monday
26

Late Summer Holiday (UK)

Tuesday
27

Wednesday
28

Thursday
29

Aug/Sep

Friday
30

Saturday
31

Al Hijra

Sunday
1

Notes

Monday
2

Tuesday
3

Wednesday
4

Thursday
5

September

Friday
6

Saturday
7

Sunday
8

Notes

Monday
9

Tuesday
10

Wednesday
11

Thursday
12

September

Friday
13

Saturday
14

Sunday
15

Notes

Monday
16

Tuesday
17

Wednesday
18

Thursday
19

September

Friday
20

Saturday
21

The United Nations International Day of Peace

Sunday
22

Notes

Monday
23

Tuesday
24

Wednesday
25

Thursday
26

September

Friday
27

Saturday
28
Anjali Shetty's Birthday

Sunday
29

Notes

October

To do...

Don't forget...

Notes...

Monday
30

Rosh Hashanah (Jewish New Year)

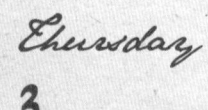

Tuesday
1

Wednesday
2

Thursday
3

Sep / Oct

Friday
4

Saturday
5

Sunday
6

Notes

Monday
7

Tuesday
8

Wednesday
9

Yom Kippur (Day of Atonement)

Thursday
10

October

Friday
11

Saturday
12

Sunday
13

Notes

Monday
14

Tuesday
15

Wednesday
16

Thursday
17

October

Friday
18

Saturday
19

Sunday
20

Notes

Monday
21

Tuesday
22

Wednesday
23

Thursday
24

October

Friday
25

Saturday
26

Sunday
27

Diwali / Daylight Saving Ends

Notes

November

To do...

Don't forget...

Notes...

Monday
28

Holiday (Republic of Ireland)

Tuesday
29

Wednesday
30

Thursday
31

Halloween

Oct / Nov

Friday
1

Saturday
2

Sunday
3

Notes

Monday
4

Tuesday
5

Guy Fawkes Night
Wednesday
6

Thursday
7

November

Friday
8

Saturday
9

Sunday
10

Remembrance Sunday

Notes

Monday
11

Tuesday
12

Wednesday
13

Thursday
14

November

Friday
15

Saturday
16

Sunday
17

Notes

Monday
18

Tuesday
19

Wednesday
20

Thursday
21

November

Friday
22

Saturday
23

Sunday
24

Notes

December

To do...

Don't forget...

Notes...

Monday
25

Tuesday
26

Wednesday
27

Thursday
28

Nov/Dec

Friday
29

Saturday
30

St. Andrew's Day (Scotland)

Sunday
1

Notes

Monday
2

Tuesday
3

Wednesday
4

Thursday
5

December

Friday
6

Saturday
7

Sunday
8

Notes

Monday
9

Tuesday
10

Wednesday
11

Thursday
12

December

Friday
13

Saturday
14

Sunday
15

Notes

Monday
16

Tuesday
17

Wednesday
18

Thursday
19

My Friends

Name:
....

Address:
....
....

Tel:
....

Mob:
....

Email:
....

Name:
....

Address:
....
....

Tel:
....

Mob:
....

Email:
....

Name:
....

Address:
....
....

Tel:
....

Mob:
....

Email:
....

Name:
....

Address:
....
....

Tel:
....

Mob:
....

Email:
....

My Friends

Name:

Address:

Tel:

Mob:

Email:

Name:

Address:

Tel:

Mob:

Email:

Breakfast — Milk with Cornflakes (6:00 – 9:00)
Boiled Eggs.
Tea.

Snack — Fruits (10:00 – 2:00)

Lunch — (3:00 – 7:00) Salad
Chapatti / Bhaji
Soup

Dinner — (? — 8:00)

Notes

Notes

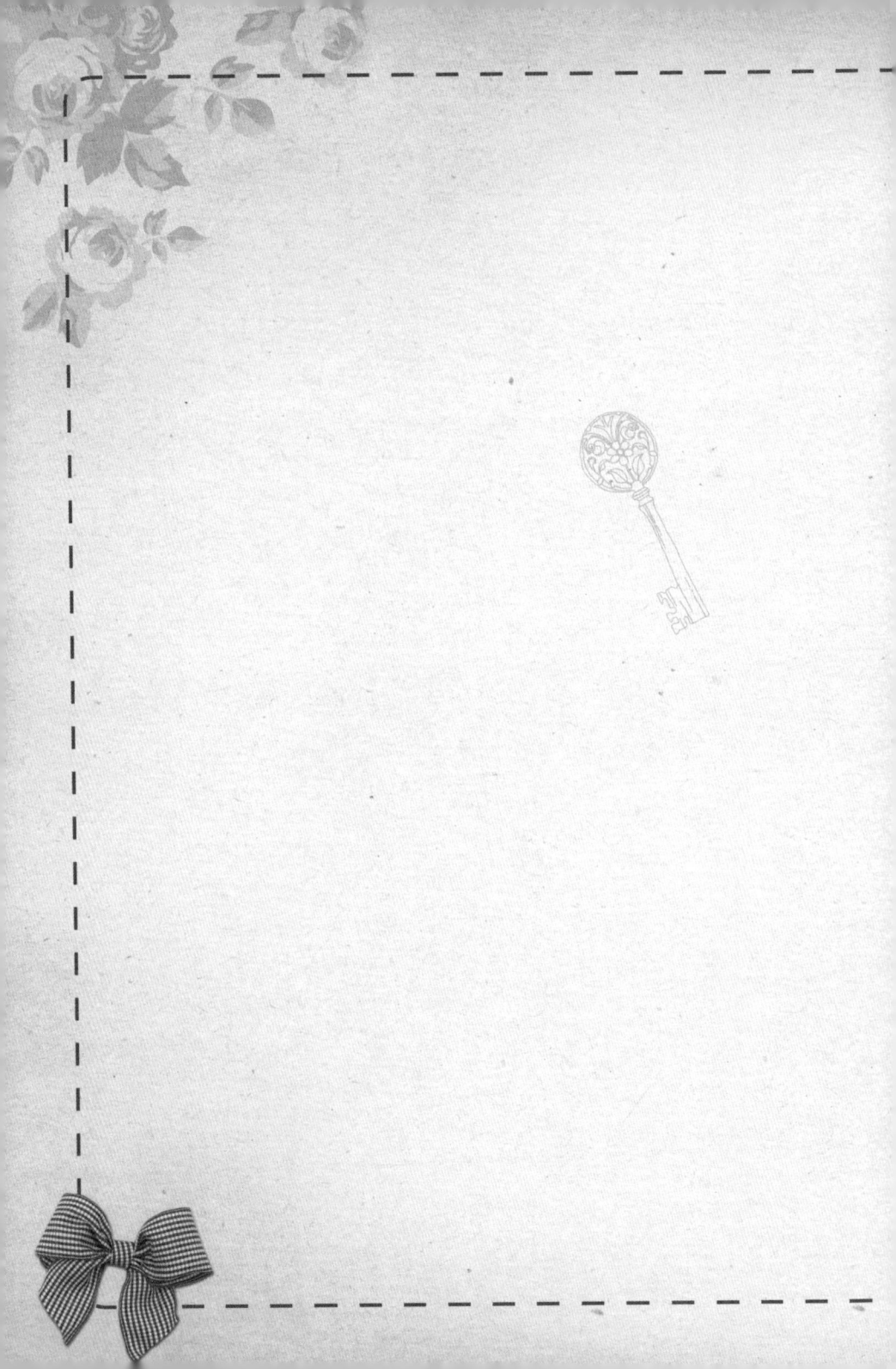

Notes

2020

January
m	t	w	t	f	s	s
		1	2	3	4	5
6	7	8	9	10	11	12
13	14	15	16	17	18	19
20	21	22	23	24	25	26
27	28	29	30	31		

February
m	t	w	t	f	s	s
					1	2
3	4	5	6	7	8	9
10	11	12	13	14	15	16
17	18	19	20	21	22	23
24	25	26	27	28	29	

March
m	t	w	t	f	s	s
						1
2	3	4	5	6	7	8
9	10	11	12	13	14	15
16	17	18	19	20	21	22
23	24	25	26	27	28	29
30	31					

April
m	t	w	t	f	s	s
		1	2	3	4	5
6	7	8	9	10	11	12
13	14	15	16	17	18	19
20	21	22	23	24	25	26
27	28	29	30			

May
m	t	w	t	f	s	s
				1	2	3
4	5	6	7	8	9	10
11	12	13	14	15	16	17
18	19	20	21	22	23	24
25	26	27	28	29	30	31

June
m	t	w	t	f	s	s
1	2	3	4	5	6	7
8	9	10	11	12	13	14
15	16	17	18	19	20	21
22	23	24	25	26	27	28
29	30					

July
m	t	w	t	f	s	s
		1	2	3	4	5
6	7	8	9	10	11	12
13	14	15	16	17	18	19
20	21	22	23	24	25	26
27	28	29	30	31		

August
m	t	w	t	f	s	s
					1	2
3	4	5	6	7	8	9
10	11	12	13	14	15	16
17	18	19	20	21	22	23
24	25	26	27	28	29	30
31						

September
m	t	w	t	f	s	s
	1	2	3	4	5	6
7	8	9	10	11	12	13
14	15	16	17	18	19	20
21	22	23	24	25	26	27
28	29	30				

October
m	t	w	t	f	s	s
			1	2	3	4
5	6	7	8	9	10	11
12	13	14	15	16	17	18
19	20	21	22	23	24	25
26	27	28	29	30	31	

November
m	t	w	t	f	s	s
						1
2	3	4	5	6	7	8
9	10	11	12	13	14	15
16	17	18	19	20	21	22
23	24	25	26	27	28	29
30						

December
m	t	w	t	f	s	s
	1	2	3	4	5	6
7	8	9	10	11	12	13
14	15	16	17	18	19	20
21	22	23	24	25	26	27
28	29	30	31			

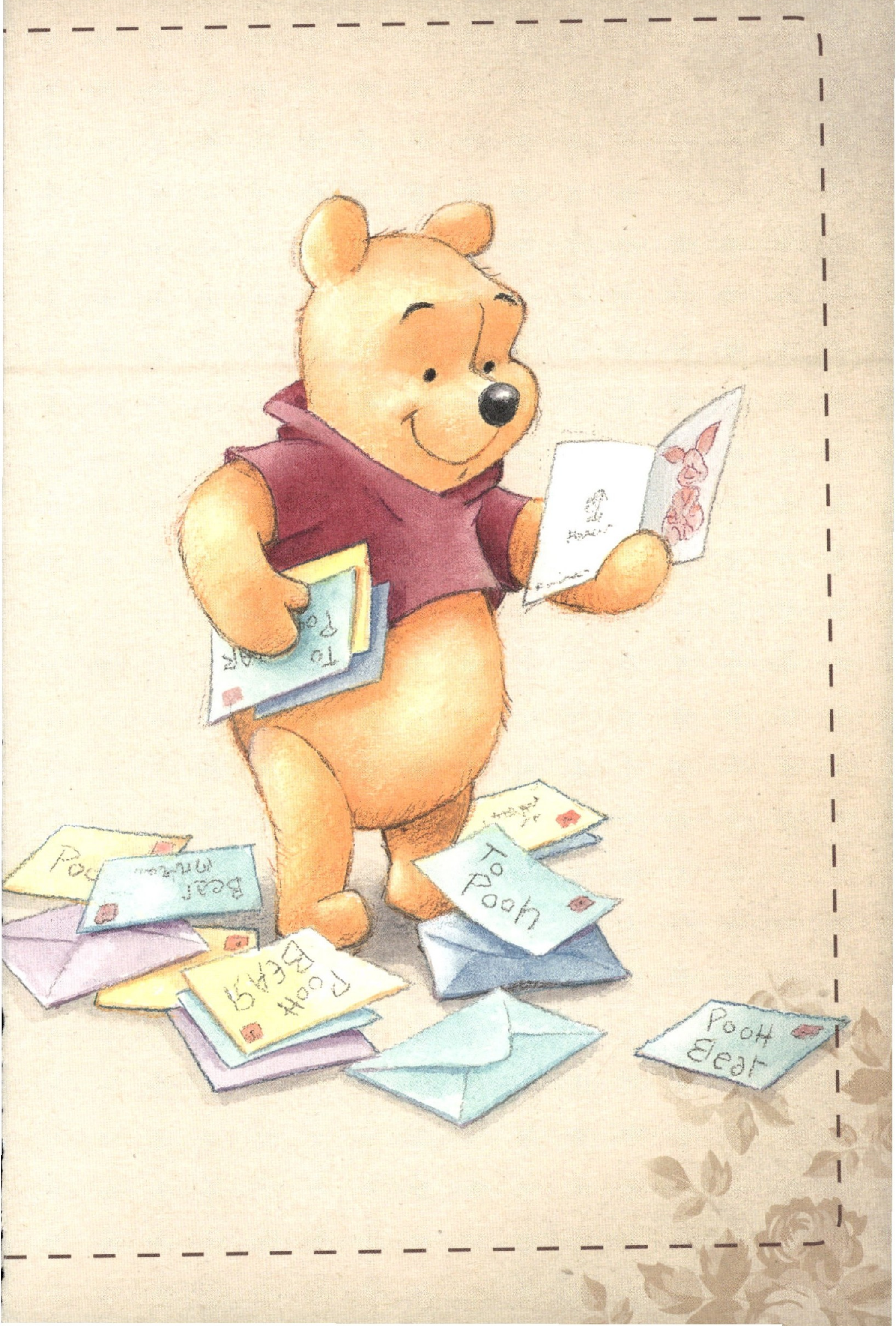
To Pooh

N	A	T	A	S	H
	B	R	O		W	N
		R				
			O			
				W	
B	R